Featherstone

50

fantastic ideas for
exploring number

ALISON HUTCHISON

Featherstone
An imprint of Bloomsbury Publishing Plc

50 Bedford Square
London
WC1B 3DP
UK

1385 Broadway
New York
NY 10018
USA

www.bloomsbury.com

FEATHERSTONE and the Feather logo are trademarks of Bloomsbury Publishing Plc

First published in Great Britain 2018

A catalogue record for this book is available from the British Library.

ISBN
PB: 978-1-4729-4864-9
ePDF: 978-1-4729-4865-6

2 4 6 8 10 9 7 5 3 1

Printed and bound in India by Replika Press Pvt. Ltd.

This book is produced using paper that is made from wood grown in managed, sustainable forests. It is natural,
renewable and recyclable. The logging and manufacturing processes conform to the environmental regulations of the
country of origin.

To find out more about our authors and books visit www.bloomsbury.com. Here you will find extracts, author interviews,
details of forthcoming events and the option to sign up for our newsletters.

Contents

Introduction 4

Counting forwards and back

Shout count.. 6

Pendulum 7

Hopping along.. 8

Songs and rhymes 10

Next three... 11

How many altogether?

Bead drop... 12

Grab.. 13

DIY dominoes... 14

Colour count.. 15

I wonder how many 16

Spotty numbers... 18

Identifying numbers

Here, there and everywhere 19

Number detectives 20

Digit sort 22

Fastest first... 23

Pipe cleaner digits....................................... 24

In pieces 25

Create in clay... 26

Making sets

Dice decides.. 27

Let's compare.. 28

Active count 29

Number tree 30

Writing numbers

Formation station 32

Newsprint digits 33

Number track games.................................... 34

Spinner bingo 36

Comparing and sequencing

Birthday line... 37

Balancing... 38

Take two 39

Guess my number 40

Counting caterpillar 41

Bead-string bag... 42

Number stories

Is that a fact?... 44

Cover it 45

Domino match... 46

What do you see? 48

Adding and taking away

Race to the top.. 49

More, more, more.. 50

Add one, take one 51

Beanbag throw 52

Reading the signs.. 53

Empty! 54

Four in a row.. 55

Missing treasure 56

Number 10 bus.. 58

Skittles... 59

Sharing

Share it out 60

Pouring and filling.. 61

Fruit salad.. 62

Questions, questions................................... 64

Introduction

To develop a strong sense of number, young children require a wide variety of meaningful hands-on experiences. The ideas in this book are all about 'doing'. They are intended not only to stimulate the senses but to provoke talking and thinking, to provide opportunities for asking questions, making discoveries, making mistakes and making connections.

Even at a young age, children's common perception of number can be that it's something quite serious, that there is only one way to do things or one 'correct answer'. They might also think it's an area of learning that they work on independently from others and that they will find out the correct way to do things when it's shown to them. Indeed, this remains the view of many adults who didn't have a positive experience when learning about number themselves. The ideas in this book challenge these perceptions by providing a variety of opportunities for children to explore and investigate number concepts without adult support, to have lots of fun whilst playing and learning collaboratively and to talk about and share their different ideas.

The activities are not intended to be rigid; take them as a starting point and make them your own. They are flexible in that they can be adapted to suit the size of your group and the needs of the children that you are planning for. The materials required for each activity have been selected for their simplicity and availability; however, in most instances these can be substituted for similar materials that you have to hand, or for something that is of more relevance or interest to your particular group.

Whilst in this early stage of learning it is vital that children have time to explore number through familiar experiences and to do activities and play games. Making number clear and accessible in this way ensures that all children, particularly those who may have formed the opinion very early on that number is not for them, develop confidence and a real 'give it a go' approach.

Pack away the flashcards and enjoy shouting, singing, creating and building the way to better number knowledge!

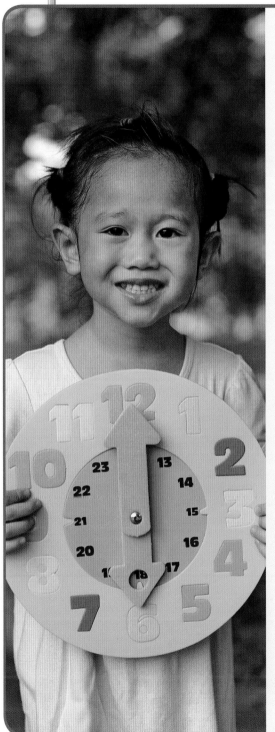

The structure of the book

The content is divided into nine sections, each focussing on a different aspect of mathematical enquiry. The pages are all organised in the same way. Before you start any activity, read through everything on the page so you are familiar with the whole activity and what you might need to plan in advance.

What you need lists the resources required for the activity. These are likely to be readily available in most settings or can be bought/made easily.

What to do tells you step-by-step what you need to do to compete the activity.

The **Health & Safety** tips are often obvious, but safety can't be overstressed. In many cases there are no specific hazards involved in completing the activity, and your usual health and safety measures should be enough. In others there are particular issues to be noted and addressed.

Taking it forward gives ideas for additional activities on the same theme, or for developing the activity further. These will be particularly useful for things that have gone especially well or where children show a real interest. In many cases they use the same resources, and in every case they have been designed to extend learning and broaden the children's experiences.

Finally, **What's in it for the children?** tells you (and others) briefly how the suggested activities contribute to learning.

Shout count
Counting forwards and back

What you need:

- Large number line display (if desired)

Top tip

If the counting becomes too loud, immediately switch to having the children take a turn to whisper. This works well when counting for the final time, as it quietens the children in preparation to move on from this activity.

What's in it for the children?

This is a great way to practise reciting the number names, to count on from and back to zero. It is also a fun way to introduce continuing the count on or back from different numbers along a boundary. The opportunity to use loud voices indoors immediately stimulates interest and excitement, and counting in this way as part of a larger group often gives less confident children motivation to join in, as they are carried along in the excitement of calling out.

Taking it forward

- Pointing to a displayed number line during the activity provides an opportunity to relate number names to their written form and reinforces each number's position in the sequence.

- Invite individual children to take the lead in this activity whilst you observe.

- Use this activity to introduce counting in steps of two, five and ten.

What to do:

1. Explain to the children that you are going to take turns to count together.

2. Ask them if they would like to whisper or shout when it is their turn to say a number. They will almost always seize the opportunity to shout!

3. Begin counting by taking turns to whisper and shout each number in the sequence. Where you count to will depend on the experience of the children. You may be counting to five, ten, or beyond.

4. Once the children are familiar with counting forwards and back from and to zero, begin counting forwards and back from different numbers along your selected number boundary.

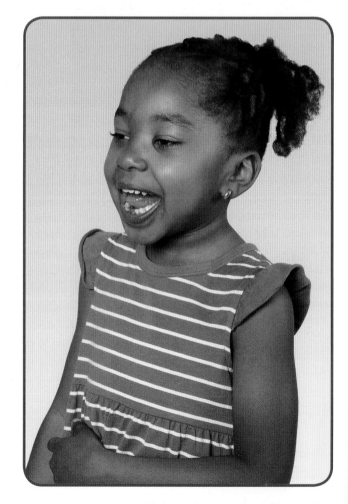

Pendulum
Counting forwards and back

What you need:

- A ball (select one with a little weight to it)
- Length of string or ribbon

Top tip ⭐

There are two options when swinging the pendulum: counting one at either side of the swing, or counting a swing back and forth as one. Which you choose will depend on the experience and confidence of the children.

What's in it for the children?

This activity provides an opportunity to practise counting forwards using number names. The swings of the pendulum reinforces the idea of counting on one after another without providing concrete objects that can be touched, moved and recounted. Inviting the children to swing the pendulum is a great way to work on coordination and control.

Taking it forward

- Provide children with pendulums to use in pairs, taking it in turn to swing or count.

- Allow access to the pendulum as a free choice activity; children often enjoy using it independently as they build their confidence with counting.

What to do:

1. Attach the ball to the length of string or ribbon to form a pendulum.

2. You may want to practise swinging the pendulum smoothly at this point, before it's used with the children.

3. Explain to the children that you are going to count together using the pendulum to help you.

4. Swing the pendulum smoothly back and forth whilst the children count in sequence.

5. Try varying the speed as the children become more confident with the activity.

6. Try asking the children to count internally without verbalising. Stop the pendulum and ask them to reveal which number they counted to; they could show this with fingers.

Hopping along
Counting forwards and back

What you need:

- Pebbles, around ten
- Permanent marker pen
- Dice
- Felt circles, around 12
  (alternatively use cork coasters)
- Small world frogs or rabbits
- Sheer green and blue silk
  or fabric (not essential)

Top tip ⭐

Take images of the children as they play to display on a whiteboard or screen. Use them to illustrate aspects of your learning goals whilst reviewing and talking about their play: 'Oh, I can see you have put the pebbles in a line and are hopping a frog along each pebble!'

What to do:

1. Mark some pebbles from 0–10 with a permanent marker pen.

2. Set out the materials without instruction for children to play with and explore within the provision.

3. Encourage the children to create games and to use the materials in different ways.

4. Join the children as they play, rolling the dice and jumping either backwards or forwards the corresponding number of spots along the circles.

5. Provide time for the children to share and discuss their play and games with the wider group. How were they using the materials? Draw out and describe the different aspects of number that were being explored.

50 fantastic ways to explore number

What's in it for the children?

This activity provides a play situation for counting small amounts and developing familiarity with jumping forwards and back along a number track. Including number pebbles and dice in an unstructured play situation is important in helping the children to recognise that using numbers can be fun. It helps to challenge the belief that there is a right or wrong way to do things with numbers if this view has begun to develop.

Taking it forward

- Explore the idea of combining two amounts within this context. If I make five jumps and then two jumps, how many jumps have I made altogether?

- Give children the opportunity to become hopping frogs or rabbits themselves by providing masks, a large dice and carpet spots.

Songs and rhymes
Counting forwards and back

What you need:

- Materials to make props

What to do:

1. There are many traditional rhymes and songs with a number focus: 'Five little speckled frogs', 'One elephant went out to play', 'Ten in a bed', 'Five little men', 'One potato, two potato'. Explore these (there are hundreds of examples online) and build up a repertoire.

2. Make accompanying props with the children. For the rhymes above, these could include: animal masks; blankets and pillows to create a bed; astronaut masks.

3. Regularly sing the songs and rhymes as a group, particularly those that involve participation.

4. Encourage the children to perform the songs and rhymes in small groups. Allow time to share performances with a wider audience.

What's in it for the children?

Repetition, rhyme, singing and actions are a great way to reinforce number names with those less familiar with the sequence. Songs that fully involve the children can provide a wonderfully interactive, visual representation of a number of objects, increasing as they are added to or decreasing as they are taken away, depending on the rhyme. They are also a great motivator for participation.

Taking it forward

- Share information about the number rhymes you have been singing with caregivers to encourage their use outside the setting.

- Provide access for the children to listen to number songs and rhymes. Encourage them to draw images to accompany these.

- Incorporate rhymes and songs tailored to the interests of the group, particular to a season/festival or linked to a specific area of learning.

Next three

Counting forwards and back

What you need:

- Large number line display (if desired)

What's in it for the children?

This activity offers the opportunity to count forwards and backwards from different points within a selected number boundary. Counting on from, or back from, is a key concept as children begin to develop understanding of adding on and taking away. Pointing to a large number line display whilst counting reinforces the relationship between number names, written numbers and their position within the number sequence.

Taking it forward

- For more experienced children, switch between counting forwards and counting backwards, whilst maintaining style and pace.

- For less experienced children, have them continue to count beyond the next three numbers, raising your hand when you wish them to stop.

What to do:

1. Explain to the children that you are going to take turns to count together.

2. Call out three numbers in sequence, e.g. five, six, seven, in a sing-song style, and have children respond by calling back the next three numbers.

3. Continue by calling out three numbers from a different starting place (don't continue on from the last three numbers).

4. Aim to continue 'call and response' in this sing-song style, maintaining a challenging pace.

5. Remember to count both forwards and backwards an equal number of times.

6. Point to and use the number line for reference whilst counting, if desired.

Bead drop
How many altogether?

What you need:

- Glass, ceramic or wooden beads
- Empty jar or metal container (something that will make a sound as a bead is dropped in)
- Large displayed number line (if desired)

Top tip

Include times where there is no sound to count.

What's in it for the children?

Through this activity, children practise using the number names in order to count how many altogether. This is a challenging activity, as whilst counting sounds, children have no visual reference to objects, nothing to hold or to move. This internal sense of number is crucial to developing number confidence. It also develops understanding that the last number counted to tells how many there are.

Taking it forward

- Use number fans or fingers to show the amount, rather than calling out.
- Ask less experienced children to keep their eyes open whilst counting; work towards eyes closed as they develop confidence.
- Use coins for this activity when introducing amounts within money.

✚ Health & Safety

Beads can be a choking hazard. Ensure appropriate supervision is in place.

What to do:

1. Hold the empty container whilst the children close their eyes, ready to count in their heads.
2. Drop the beads into the container, one at a time.
3. Ask the children to open their eyes and reveal the number of beads that they counted. 'How many altogether? How many in total?'
4. If working with a group, make comparisons between suggestions as they are made. 'That is a smaller number than the others. That's the biggest number suggested so far.'
5. Empty out the container and drop the beads back in, whilst re-counting them together to find the total.
6. Talk with the children about their amounts and the actual number of beads in the container. Highlight positives, particularly for those less confident. 'That was only one more than we have; that was very close.'
7. Varying the speed and regularity as the beads are dropped into the container alters the challenge of this activity significantly.

50 fantastic ways to explore number

Grab
How many altogether?

What you need:

- Large container
- Set of small objects (dried pasta or beans, pom-poms or buttons all work well)
- Blank ten frame grids

Top tip ⭐

Carefully selecting the size of the objects in the container will restrict the total number the children are able to grab. For greater challenge, offer smaller objects.

What's in it for the children?

During this activity, the children gain experience in seeing a group of objects and estimating the total number. Organising the objects before counting encourages greater accuracy, as each object is touched and moved as the children say the number names in sequence. This activity reinforces the idea that numbers represent quantities of real objects.

Taking it forward

- Provide materials for the children to record this activity using their own pictures and marks.

- Using smaller objects in the container is a fun way to introduce counting beyond familiar numbers. Talk with the children about adding another number frame if they grab more than ten objects. Support them as they count.

What to do:

1. Fill the container with the small objects.
2. Invite children to grab a handful of objects from the container.
3. Challenge the children to guess how many objects they have picked up.
4. Ask them to arrange the objects onto an empty grid and to count the total.
5. Encourage them to compare their guess and the actual counted number of objects. Were they close to each other?

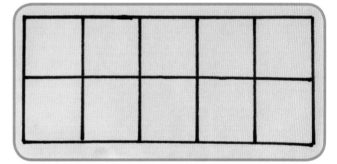

DIY dominoes

How many altogether?

What you need:

- Counters
- Dominoes
- Baskets
- White card
- Scissors
- Pen

Top tip

Do not use dominoes that have different-coloured spots for each number, or children can simply match by colour, rather than counting spots or developing pattern recognition.

What's in it for the children?

This offers an opportunity to practise counting accurately with built-in self-assessment on completion, as the dominoes are placed together for visual comparison. Through this activity, children are also developing sight recognition of domino patterns. Developing sight recognition of amounts to six without having to count is an important skill.

Taking it forward

- Have traditional sets of dominoes available in your provision and show the children how to play them independently.

- Provide paper domino templates and ask the children to create matching dominoes by drawing on the spots.

What to do:

1. Organise the counters and dominoes into separate baskets.

2. Cut the card into rectangles measuring approximately 6 cm x 12 cm.

3. Draw a black line in the centre of each rectangle and cut around the corners. You are aiming to create a blank domino card. Laminating the cards at this point will ensure that they last longer.

4. Present the dominoes, counters and blank domino cards to the children.

5. Invite the children to choose a domino, count the spots on each side, and to then use the counters and the blank domino card to create a matching domino.

6. Encourage the children to arrange the counters in exactly the same layout as the original domino dots.

7. Ask the children to put their dominoes side by side to compare and check that they are exactly the same.

Colour count

How many altogether?

What you need:

- Shallow basket
- Coloured counters or pom-poms

Top tip

Replace these materials with construction bricks or any other enticing material that could be sorted by colour. Seasonally, this could include autumn leaves or flowers.

What's in it for the children?

Sorting and making number statements in this way reinforces understanding that a number represents a quantity. The children gain experience of counting a small number of objects in a group by touching each object and saying the number names in order. Working in pairs to listen to and check a partner's number statements ensures greater accuracy and doubles the opportunities for counting practice within the activity.

Taking it forward

- Invite the children to draw pictures to represent their handfuls. Can they add numbers or personal symbols to indicate amounts?

- More experienced children can be asked to make comparisons between amounts within their handfuls whilst making their number statements.

What to do:

1. Fill the basket with the counters or pom-poms.

2. Working in pairs, invite both children to take a handful from the basket.

3. Encourage the children to sort the individual handfuls of objects by colour and then count how many objects in each colour group.

4. Ask them to take turns to make number statements about each colour to a partner. 'I have five red counters; I have three blue counters.'

5. Each statement should be checked for accuracy as the partner recounts the total number in each of the colour groups.

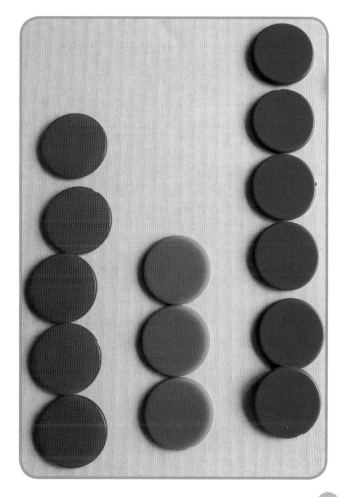

I wonder how many

How many altogether?

What you need:

- Picture cards of objects within the setting
- Whiteboard pens

Top tip

This activity has the potential to become quite disruptive, so limit the disruption by thinking ahead. Do you really want cartons of paint repeatedly taken out from the store cupboard under the sink? Think carefully about the objects on the picture cards!

What's in it for the children?

Finding out how many altogether using everyday objects in a very familiar setting immediately generates interest and discussion. It reinforces understanding that numbers are used to represent quantities, that counting how many altogether is useful and serves a purpose in our lives. In estimating the number before they check with counting, the children are developing their approximation skills and further consolidating their sense of quantity. This activity provides a unique opportunity to count a group of objects that cannot be physically moved and grouped together – something the children may not have tackled before, and something they may have to find a strategy for whilst counting.

What to do:

1. Prepare cards with images of objects within your setting that provide opportunities for the children to count how many there are altogether. Chairs, tables, windows, children, taps, paintbrushes, cupboards, scissors, books or drawers are good examples, but make yours personal to your setting.

2. Laminate the cards at this point for longer term use and to act as a recording surface for the children's findings.

3. Stimulate interest in the activity by looking through the cards and talking with the children, saying to them: 'I wonder how many windows we have in the room, how many tables…'

4. Select one card to demonstrate the activity. Choose something that cannot easily be counted from where you are gathered.

5. Before counting, ask the children to estimate how many altogether. Talk these through.

6. Choose a child to check the actual number by counting. Ask them to record the number on the card with a whiteboard pen before bringing it back and sharing with the group.

7. Encourage the children to compare their estimate to the final count. Was it close?

8. Display the cards and allow access to whiteboard pens, for the children's independent use.

9. Encourage them to work on this activity with a partner, rather than alone. Ask them to think about whether there might be different ways to count the objects, and to think and talk together to decide how they are going to find how many altogether before they begin each card.

Taking it forward

- Take time to revisit a few of the cards once the children have had time to work with them independently. Discuss the different strategies they used to count a set of objects that were not always physically grouped together. Find out how accurate their independent counting was.

- Ask the children if there are objects in the room that they would like to count that are not displayed on the cards. Invite them to create missing cards that are of interest to them.

- Widen this idea beyond the setting and beyond numbers the children are comfortably able to count. Ask the children to consider how many fish are in the sea, birds in the sky, books in the local library, people in the town, wheels in the car park. The possibilities are endless! Children will also enjoy creating their own questions. These cannot be counted, but they can be made into an interesting 'I wonder…' display.

Spotty numbers

How many altogether?

What you need:

- Blank cards approximately 6 cm x 6 cm
- Sheets of circular stickers

Top tip

Some children really enjoy the opportunity to use stickers. It is important to agree and reinforce a maximum number. Ten is given here as an example, but it really depends on the ability of the children.

What's in it for the children?

This fun activity is a great way to practise counting accurately, as the stickers are carefully counted as they are stuck down, and counted again to check how many there are. It is an opportunity to work on developing a sound sense of estimating and approximating small amounts (subitizing) as the group is glimpsed for a short time before it disappears.

Taking it forward

- Invite the children to show their cards to different partners.
- Collect the cards together and make available for independent use within your provision.
- Make a 3D version of this activity using beads/buttons/pom-poms and containers. 'Guess how many beads are inside each container?' is a great provocation for discussion.

What to do:

1. Working in pairs, each child should select five blank cards.

2. Choosing a different number from zero to ten for each card, the children can work independently to attach the corresponding number of stickers to each card.

3. Encourage the children to be creative and random in their placement of stickers.

4. Taking it in turns, the children 'flash' the cards, one at a time, for a few seconds to their partner, who calls out the number that they think is shown on the card.

5. Both children count the stickers on each card to check how many they have.

Here, there and everywhere
Identifying numbers

What you need:

* Images of numbers from different contexts beyond the setting, e.g. road signs or shop signs.

Top tip ⭐

If possible, show some recognisable images from places around the locality, such as a swimming pool, supermarket or bus stop. This immediately sparks engagement and prompts discussion.

What's in it for the children?

Regularly discussing images of real numbers from the wider world allows children to develop an awareness and understanding of different ways that numbers can be displayed and the different types of information that they help to communicate. It also allows children to begin to notice numbers themselves and to consider the many ways they may use them in their everyday lives.

Taking it forward

* Create a display of the images, along with the children's comments and ideas from the discussion.

* Encourage children to add to the display with examples of numbers they have spotted whilst out and about or within their homes.

What to do:

1. Show the images, or allow the children to explore copies of the images independently.

2. Talk with the children, exploring their ideas of where they think each image is from, why they think a number is being used, what information they think the number is showing, and what would happen if there were no numbers there.

3. Can they identify any numbers within the images?

4. Allow time to discuss children's experiences of numbers in similar situations within their day-to-day lives, for example, whilst travelling, shopping, visiting local amenities, or around the home.

Number detectives
Identifying numbers

What you need:

- Visual 'spotting' cards with digits 0–9 clearly displayed
- Digital cameras (if desired)

What to do:

1. Prepare 'spotting' cards for use during the number hunt. The size and layout of the digits on the card should be simple and clear. Laminating the cards will ensure they are more robust.

2. Go beyond your setting into the immediate indoor area on a number hunt.

3. Look closely at signs, wall displays, doorways and objects. Try to stand back and allow the children the excitement of finding numbers themselves, rather than having them 'shown' to them.

4. Encourage the children to use their digit spotting cards to identify the digits within the numbers as they find them. They may not be able to read numbers outside of their number range, but they will be able to talk about the digits that they can see.

5. Discuss some of the numbers as they are spotted. 'What are they there for? What are they telling us? What would happen if they weren't there?' – This last one is a great question!

6. Invite the children to take digital images of the numbers to create a display or book to refer to.

7. Ask them to keep spotting and to share any new numbers they find with the group.

What's in it for the children?

Often, children are encouraged to look for letters and words in their immediate environment as they begin to learn more about phonics and reading; numbers, however, are often overlooked. Becoming aware of numbers in the environment and developing an understanding of the information being communicated through numbers is an essential skill.

Taking it forward

- Encourage the children to keep looking out for numbers; make time for them to add to the display or book and share with the group.

- Invite ideas for creating signs or posters that display more numbers within the immediate environment. Identify why they are required, what they will communicate, and experiment with different styles and layouts. If more signs and labels are unnecessary (most early years settings already have many), the children could replace the existing signs/labels with ones they have created.

Digit sort
Identifying numbers

What you need:

- Variety of representations of digits 0–9
- Materials to create tactile digit cards
- Basket

Top tip ⭐

Eye-catching digits make this a really engaging task. Utilise your sewing, painting, decoupage, knitting and crafting skills, or the skills of others. Choose interesting and unusual materials.

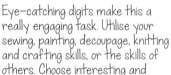

What's in it for the children?

This is an opportunity to completely focus in on the shape of each digit from 0–9. To become secure in identification, and as they begin forming numbers themselves, children must have experience of identifying numbers in a wide range of formats. Including examples of reversals builds awareness, and again becomes useful as children begin to record numbers themselves.

Taking it forward

- Refresh this activity with examples focusing on numbers that individuals may be struggling to identify consistently.
- Provide materials for the children to make examples of their own for others to sort.

What to do:

1. Gather together a wide variety of different representations of digits 0–9. Find these in magazines and newspapers, on packaging and displays. Include differences in style, size and colour. Display these individually, one digit per card.

2. Create cards with tactile digits using materials such as bubble wrap, foil, fabric, and found natural materials and craft supplies.

3. Work along with the children with the digits or invite the children to explore them independently.

4. Challenge the children to sort the digits into groups from 0–9.

5. Ensure the children are correctly naming each digit at this point, not reinforcing misconceptions or errors and not leaving gaps in their knowledge with unknown digits.

6. Include examples of digits that are not easily identified; make examples that do not have the correct formation to provide discussion, such as the reversal of a digit.

Fastest first

What you need:

- Length of plain paper
- Pens
- White card
- Container or basket
- Counters
- Length of table-top or floor space with access at both sides

Top tip

Using an adult as the caller in this activity creates a great assessment opportunity.

What's in it for the children?

This is a game to develop number recognition that includes an element of competition. Many number games that help to consolidate learning involve an element of competition; they offer a great opportunity to work on resilience and awareness of other's emotions.

Taking it forward

- Change the game by using different number boundaries; simplify by using 0–5; extend by using 0–20 or beyond.

- If children require support to identify the numbers, invite the caller to show the selected card to both players.

What to do:

1. Using tape, secure a length of the paper (around one metre) down the centre of a table (or on a floor space).

2. Write the numbers 0–10 randomly along the length of the paper on both sides.

3. Make a set of 'caller cards' by cutting card into squares and writing the numbers 0–10 on them. Put the cards in a container.

4. Invite two children to play 'fastest first' and another child to call the numbers.

5. Stand the players at either side of the table and the caller, with the caller cards and counters, at one end.

6. The aim of the game is to be the fastest to point to the corresponding number called by the caller as cards are drawn from the container. 'Fastest first' collects a counter.

7. The first to collect five counters wins the game!

Pipe cleaner digits

Identifying numbers

What you need:

- **Extra-long pipe cleaners**
- **Digit cards 0–9**

What's in it for the children?

Concentrating on each digit in this way reinforces the relationship between number names and their written form. It also develops the familiarity of shape and form required for writing numbers.

Taking it forward

- Invite children to thread a number of beads onto the pipe cleaner before shaping the corresponding digit.

- Challenge more experienced children to use a length of ribbon or wool to shape digits on a flat surface.

- Provide threading cards shaped as digits and laces as a complementary experience.

What to do:

1. Provide the pipe cleaners and digit cards for independent use.

2. Demonstrate how to shape a pipe cleaner into a digit.

3. Encourage the use of one pipe cleaner per digit or as few per digit as possible. If lots are used, the digits become very difficult to identify amongst the joins and twists.

4. Challenge the children to shape and create different digits using the pipe cleaners.

5. Create a display with the numbers. They look good hanging up.

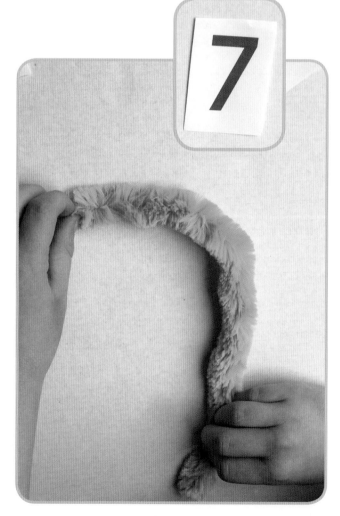

In pieces

What you need:

- Strong card
- Scissors
- Pencil
- Broad marker pen
- Digit cards 0–9

What to do:

1. Cut ten pieces of card, approximately A3 in size.
2. Sketch the outline of each digit from 0–9, one per card.
3. Cut around each digit.
4. Use the marker to boldly outline each digit just inside the outside edge.
5. You are now aiming to create a jigsaw from each digit.
6. Decide how many pieces to cut each digit into. The greater the number of pieces, the more complex this activity becomes.
7. Gather together all of the jigsaw pieces in a basket, along with the digit cards for reference.
8. Invite the children to piece together each digit.

What's in it for the children?

Children get to work on a different aspect of number recognition, as this activity calls for the recall of the shapes that combine to make up each digit. This is particularly challenging if completed without the visual aid of a number card. Completing this problem-solving challenge in pairs or small groups generates valuable discussion.

Taking it forward

- Simplify this activity by limiting the number of digits presented at any one time.
- Invite the children to create their own digit jigsaws by drawing a digit in the centre of a rectangular piece of plain paper and cutting it into pieces. Can a friend put their jigsaw together?

Create in clay
Identifying numbers

What you need:

- Air-drying clay
- Mats
- Water
- Clay tools
- Plastic magnetic digits 0–9
- Space for the clay to dry
- Paints
- Paintbrushes
- PVA glue

Top tip

The digits could also be made with salt dough and baked to dry them out before being painted and sealed.

What's in it for the children?

This tactile experience is a great way to work on number recognition. It expands the children's sense of the shape of each number, which informs written number formation as they move on to this stage.

Taking it forward

- Use the finished digits to create beautifully tactile number lines.
- Put the finished digits into a feely bag and play guess the number.

What to do:

1. Set up a working area for the clay with mats, water and clay tools.
2. Add the magnetic digits to the area, ensuring there are multiple examples of each.
3. Show the children how to create a digit from a ball of clay.
4. Emphasise careful replication of curves and straights.
5. Invite the children to create their own clay digits.
6. Allow the children to display a few of their numbers in a predetermined space. These will remain in the space until they are fully dried. Some children may want to keep all of their numbers, so it's important that you discuss this beforehand if you wish to limit the number that each child can save to dry.
7. Paint the dry numbers and coat with PVA glue to seal.

What you need:

- Dice (with spots)
- Small items for counting
- Blank ten frames

Top tip

Try to select objects that will appeal to the children. Shiny materials always generate interest, and natural materials work well, e.g. pebbles, shells and small cones.

What's in it for the children?

Young children need many experiences of counting out a small number of objects from a larger group in order to develop accuracy. This simple activity focuses on developing a successful strategy for counting, through moving each item, touching and arranging in place within a ten frame.

Taking it forward

- Work alongside less experienced children and model the counting process.

- For more experienced children, offer either a dice marked with digits or a 0–9 number spinner; or customise a blank dice to meet their requirements.

- Ask more experienced children to work out 'How many more to make ten?'.

What to do:

1. Provide the children with dice and a selection of small items for counting.

2. Ask them to roll the dice and count out the corresponding number of items.

3. Encourage them to organise the items into their blank ten frames, saying each number in sequence as each item is added to the frame.

4. Finally, ask the children to recount the items as a total number, checking it was the total that they set out to create, before they clear their ten frames and roll the dice again.

5. Observing the children and talking with them as they undertake this activity provides great assessment information.

Let's compare

What you need:

- Sets of materials with large differences in size; use familiar items from your immediate environment
- Number cards from 0–10

What to do:

1. Arrange the sets of materials or objects within their storage containers ready for use.
2. Working alongside the children, invite a child to select a number card.
3. Ask the children to select one material and count out a set that matches the number card.
4. Make a few sets of the same number with different materials. Encourage differences in size between each set: tiny beads, large construction blocks, slim lolly sticks.
5. Once a few sets showing the same total number of objects has been created, ask the children which is biggest/smallest or which has most/least.
6. Talk with the children about their ideas and observations, arriving at the conclusion that no matter what size of objects used, each set has the same number of objects.

What's in it for the children?

This experience allows children to explore the concept that it is the total number of items in a collection that determines the size of a set, and that this total number is not dependent on the physical size or shape of the items. Visually comparing a set of five large objects with a set of five tiny objects whilst recognising, and understanding that they are the same in numerical terms, can be very challenging for some children.

Taking it forward

- Introduce and use the term 'equal' during this activity.
- Try discussing examples within the wider environment, for example: five ladybirds/five buses; two trees/two leaves.

Active count

What you need:

- Large dice with plastic pockets and plain card, or wipeable dice
- Fibre-tip pens
- Dice (with spots)

What to do:

1. Draw parts of the body, either directly onto the blank dice or onto cards to insert into the pockets on the dice Head, legs with feet, one whole body, hands, two bodies and a mouth will work well.

2. Working with the children, explain that you are going to roll both dice. The spotty dice will determine how many actions are made; the second dice will determine which part of the body is used. When 'two bodies' shows on the dice, the children have to complete the action with a partner.

3. Talk with the children each time about possible actions, and agree on one that everyone is going to use: hand clapping, spinning around, stomping.

4. Ensure the children complete the actions at the same time; inaccuracies stand out clearly when counting together in sync.

What's in it for the children?

In this activity, children count a set number without having something permanent to refer to. Creating a movement whilst counting in sequence can be a real challenge for some children; stopping at the correct number can take lots of practice.

Taking it forward

- Share this idea with caregivers; it's a fun physical activity to practise counting at home.

- Make the dice available for children to use independently within the provision.

Number tree

What you need:

- Small branches
- Vase or vessel
- Card
- Scissors
- Hole punch
- Ribbon
- Mini pegs

What to do:

1. Arrange the branches in a vase or other vessel to create a small tree.

2. Using the card, cut out 30 leaf shapes approximately 5 cm in length.

3. Punch a hole at the top of each leaf.

4. Thread a length of ribbon approximately 8 cm through each hole; tie off to form a loop.

5. Mark each leaf in the centre with a number from 1–10; do this three times for each number.

6. Put the number leaves and pegs in separate containers.

7. Present the materials to the children alongside the small tree.

8. Ask the children to decorate the 'number tree'.

9. Children select a leaf, count out and attach the corresponding number of pegs to their leaf, then hang it on the tree.

10. Working alongside children, ask, 'What happens if you move the pegs on your leaf around to a different place?' Physically move the pegs as you ask, 'What if we put two pegs here and two pegs here, or three pegs here and one peg there?'

11. Discuss ideas and investigate changing the position of pegs by partitioning each number in different ways. Count aloud together, checking that the total number has stayed the same.

12. Does the way that the pegs are positioned on the leaf make a difference to how many there are altogether?

What's in it for the children?

When challenged to move the pegs to different positions, children discover that the number of objects within a set does not change if it is moved around or partitioned in different ways; it remains the same. This is a great fine motor workout, as the children work to attach the small pegs and hang each number onto the tree.

Taking it forward

- Simplify this activity by reducing the numbers on the leaves to 1–5.

- When the tree is full, rather than doing it yourself, ask the children to remove the numbers from the tree, carefully counting the pegs for accuracy as they replace the materials in the containers.

Formation station

Writing numbers

What you need:

- Wide variety of mark-making materials: fibre-tip pens, wax crayons, chalks, highlighters, finger paint, dry wipe board markers

- Variety of surfaces; paper, chalkboards, dry wipe boards, foil, fabric, textured card

- Digit cards 0–9

- Space for a display wall

Top tip ⭐

There will be vast differences in initial attempts at digit formation, depending on experience. Regularly clear the display area to stop it becoming a showcase for the more experienced, and target support at less experienced children to ensure their attempts are valued and displayed too.

What's in it for the children?

Through this activity, children begin their mark-making journey with digits. The emphasis at this stage is on 'having a go' and having fun. Providing a display area encourages children to use self-evaluation and to recognise and share their achievements.

Taking it forward

- Provide shallow trays filled with dry sand, foam or glitter for multisensory formation practice.

- Use the formation station area to target specific digits that are causing children difficulty with reversal or formation.

What to do:

1. Set up a 'number formation station' with a variety of mark-making materials, different surfaces and clearly displayed digit cards from 0–9.

2. Prepare a blank wall display space close to the area, at child height if possible.

3. Demonstrate the formation of each digit for the children.

4. Encourage the children to create each digit using a variety of materials.

5. Do not impose restrictions or rules around material selection at this stage, as some less confident children may choose to use semi-permanent materials such as a whiteboard or chalk to begin with.

6. Talk to the children about the importance of correct formation and encourage them to check for reversals as they form the digits.

7. Ask the children to self-select examples of their digits to add to the wall display for others to see.

Newsprint digits

What you need:

- Supply of old newspaper pages
- Number magnets
- Broad fibre-tip pens

Top tip

To encourage really reluctant children to have a go with each digit, emphasise the transient nature of this material and activity by scribbling over some of your less successful digits as you model the process, encouraging them to do the same.

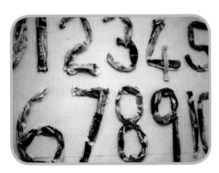

What's in it for the children?

This activity combines number recognition practice with number formation as the digits are brought to life. The nature of the materials being re-used in this activity, and a knowledge that the paper is going to be shaped into a wall display concealing their mark making, can help to free the children to 'have a go' at each digit.

Taking it forward

- Invite the children to use floor space to construct giant digits by reusing recyclable bottles or cartons.

What to do:

1. Lay out the newspaper pages and magnetic digits for visual reference along table tops. (Broadsheets work well.)

2. Encourage the children to use the pens to cover the newspaper sheets in digits.

3. Ask them to try drawing each digit ten times.

4. Ask them to select the digit that they are happiest with, draw a circle around it and share it with a friend.

5. Encourage digits in different sizes; really large numbers look very impressive.

6. Now demonstrate how to use the newspaper sheets to twist and shape a number. Lay component parts onto the table if necessary to create the number. Ask the children to check for accuracy.

7. Invite the children to twist, roll, and shape the sheets that they have written on to create their own 3D digits.

8. Create a wall display of the digits, using wall staples to secure different parts in place.

Number track games

What you need:

- Examples of number games with a track format
- Blank number track templates
- Dice or spinners
- Counters

Top tip

Ensure that the number of squares on the blank track templates fall within the number boundaries that the children are working on recording independently.

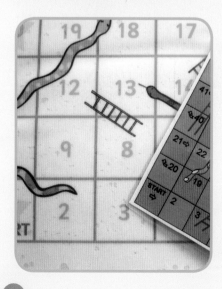

What to do:

1. Prepare blank paper track templates in advance, using either A4 or A3 size paper. A3 works well for pairs; A4 is best for independent work. It's easiest to draw these freehand and photocopy the required amount.

2. Spend time playing with number track games such as Snakes and Ladders. These can be handmade or purchased; there are many examples on the market.

3. Talk with the children about the format and layout of the games. Establish that they each use a marked number track for players to move along.

4. Find out opinions of the games; identify likes and dislikes.

5. Working with the children, create a simple track game on a large sheet of plain paper, or on a whiteboard.

6. Generate ideas for possible themes; encourage personalisation and creativity. Draw small illustrations on and around the track to make it attractive and give it a theme.

7. Using the games that have been played as a reference, identify words that may also be required on the track: start, finish, skip, go back/forward, move, miss. Write these on to the track.

8. Come up with a name for the new game.

9. Using the game that has been created as an example, discuss and identify simple success criteria for a completed game.

10. Challenge the children to work independently or in pairs to create a track game using a blank track template. Support as required.

11. Ensure that the children check the numbers on their track for accuracy, both for correct formation and correct sequence. It's easy for numbers to be missed out in the excitement of creating a game!

12. Enjoy playing the games that have been created.

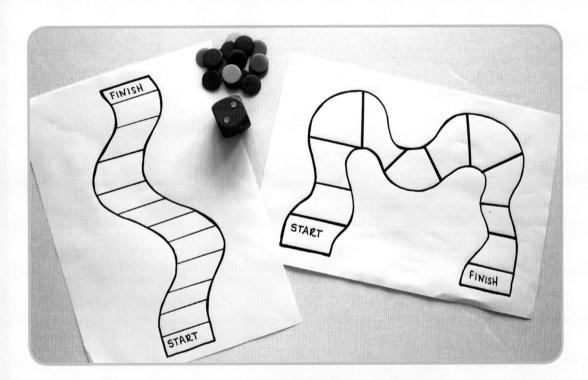

What's in it for the children?

This activity provides a fun opportunity for children to practise writing numbers in the correct sequence with a real purpose. The children will learn from experience that for a track game to be successful and enjoyable, the numbers must be clear and legible.

Taking it forward

- Laminate completed games for on-going use in the provision.

- For less experienced children, provide numbers to be attached onto the track, ensuring they can still participate in this activity whilst they refine their digit formation skills. Sheets of stickers work well for this.

- Provide ongoing access to blank number tracks for future use. Children enjoy returning to this activity with different ideas.

Spinner bingo
Writing numbers

What you need:

- Blank grids, 3 squares by 3 squares
- Pens
- Number spinner 0–9
- Coloured counters

Taking it forward.

- Once familiar with the game format, invite children to complete and then swap bingo cards before the game begins.
- Pre-make the bingo cards with numbers already selected and written on, changing the emphasis of this activity to number recognition.
- Return to this game once the children have an understanding of larger numbers and addition. Select nine numbers between two and 18. Use two number spinners and cover the total.

What to do:

1. Invite the children to play this game in pairs or a small group.
2. Give a blank grid to each child.
3. Ask the children to write a number between zero and nine in each square of the blank grid.
4. Explain that each number can be written many times, and that all of the numbers from zero to nine do not need to be represented on the grid. The final selection of numbers is entirely their choice. Build the excitement at this point! Once completed, this becomes their bingo card.
5. Taking it in turns, the children each spin the number spinner, using the counters to cover the numbers on their card (if generated by the spinner during their turn).
6. When all nine numbers on a card are covered with a counter, we have a bingo winner!

What's in it for the children?

This game combines an opportunity to match number names to their written form and to practise writing numbers with a real purpose. It also begins to develop awareness of chance and likelihood.

Birthday line
Comparing and sequencing

What you need:

- Birthday cards showing numbers 1–10
- Pegs
- Baskets or containers
- Resources to create a washing line

What's in it for the children?

The children get to use a fun, familiar context to develop number order and sequencing knowledge. As children create their number line, they are thinking about and checking the number that comes before and after. It is also an opportunity to consolidate knowledge of number orientation, as each birthday card number should be pegged onto the line the correct way up.

Taking it forward

- Talk with the children about their ages. 'How old were you before your last birthday? How old will you be next birthday?' Ask about the ages of relatives and friends; many children will be aware of special birthdays e.g. 40, 50, 60.

- Use this as a 'what's missing?' activity – peg up a line with cards missing, inviting the children to identify and fill in the missing numbers.

- Take the birthday theme further by inflating and sequencing numbered birthday balloons.

What to do:

1. Organise the cards and pegs in containers.
2. Set up a washing line at child height.
3. Ensure that it is firmly secured and in a safe place that is not a pathway within your space.
4. Invite the children to peg up the birthday cards to create a number line.
5. Can they sequence them from smallest to largest?
6. Can they sequence them from largest to smallest?

Top tip

Once complete, ask children to find a friend to take a picture of themselves and their number line with a digital camera, providing you both with a visual reference of their work before it disappears.

Balancing
Comparing and sequencing

What you need:

- Wooden blocks
- Basket
- Clipboard
- Grid for recording

Top tip

This activity can draw out a sense of competition – use it as an opportunity to encourage sensitivity and teamwork.

What to do:

1. Set this activity up as an independent challenge.

2. Arrange the blocks in a basket.

3. Use paper to prepare a recording grid with a space for the children to write their name in one column alongside the number of blocks they have balanced in another. Attach this to a clipboard.

4. Create a simple sign asking the children: 'How many blocks can you balance?'

5. Explain the challenge to the children, showing them how to record using the grid.

6. After a period of time being independently used, plan time as a group to reflect on responses to the challenge.

7. Identify the largest number of blocks that were balanced. Talk about which numbers were closest to this.

8. How many children balanced more than five or ten blocks?

9. Talk with the children about the different ways that the number of blocks being balanced could be increased. (This challenge does not ask them to build a tower.)

What's in it for the children?

This is a fun, practical challenge to encourage number comparison. Use this opportunity to widen number language, including: largest, highest, smallest, more than, less than, nearly, and closest to.

Taking it forward

- Use a different material: anything that will stack or balance.

- Create similar opportunities with a comparative focus: 'How many spots can you paint onto this sheet of paper? How many jumps can you make before the sand timer runs out?'

Take two
Comparing and sequencing

What you need:

- Container or basket
- Small items for scooping (beads, dried butter beans, pom-poms or buttons all work well)
- Scoops

What to do:

1. Fill a container with the objects. This activity works best if it's really full and the children can get a good-sized scoop from the container.
2. Model this activity for the children.
3. Take two scoops from the container, one at a time; lay each scoop out separately onto a flat surface.
4. How many items do we guess are in each scoop?
5. Count out the number of items in each scoop, organising them side by side for comparison.
6. Talk with the children and make comparisons between the number in each scoop: 'Were they the same/equal? Which was biggest/smallest? Which had most/least?'
7. Try with another two scoops; model the process once more. Discuss the numbers in these two scoops, compared to the first two. 'Will the amounts always be different?'
8. Invite the children to explore the activity.
9. Work alongside them, reinforcing the language of comparison.

What's in it for the children?

This offers an opportunity to count out and compare two amounts in terms of the same/equal, bigger/smaller, more and less. Depending on the size of the items, the number of items scooped may go beyond the numbers that the children can comfortably write or recognise, but are within their oral counting range. It's important to stretch them in this way, as number knowledge is continually expanding.

Taking it forward

- Include discussion of 'the difference between' for more confident children.
- Provide different-sized scoops. Encourage investigation of the number of items different sizes can hold.
- Invite the children to use their own marks, pictures, words or numbers to record the activity.

Guess my number
Comparing and sequencing

What you need:

- Magnetic numbers from 0–9
- Magnetic display board

What's in it for the children?

This game reinforces number recognition and helps children construct relevant questions while providing practice, reinforcement, and application of comparative number language. Playing in a group ensures that less experienced children gain from hearing more sophisticated questions than they themselves may have asked.

Taking it forward

- Limit the number of questions that can be asked within one game. If the chosen number is reached before the correct number is guessed, then the person selecting the number becomes the winner.

- Revisit the game once children have an understanding of different areas of number (such as add and take away). This increases the range of questions that can be asked.

- Create 'Who am I?'-style number riddles to read and solve with the children.

What to do:

1. Display the numbers randomly on the board, ensuring that each child can see them.

2. Explain to the children that you have chosen one of the numbers. Can they guess which one?

3. Without experience of this activity, children will suggest numbers; they will not ask questions. Allow this initially, moving numbers to the side as they are incorrectly guessed, until only the correct number remains.

4. Explain to the children that they can ask questions to help them to guess the number.

5. Suggest some examples of questions that could be asked: 'Is it bigger than/smaller than, more than/less than, does it come before/after, does it come between?'

6. Play the game again. Inviting questions, model the elimination process, talking and thinking aloud as each question is applied to the remaining numbers.

7. Provide the children with a set of magnetic numbers and board to enable them to play the game independently (in pairs or small groups).

8. You may choose to record the questions being used as a reference for play in the future.

Counting caterpillar

Comparing and sequencing

What you need:

- Paints
- Paintbrushes
- Large gummed paper circles
- Number cards 0–10

Top tip

Use shades of favourite colours, metallic paints or sparkly paints to make this as fun and engaging as possible, increasing the likelihood that the caterpillar will be displayed at home.

What's in it for the children?

This activity provides a fun opportunity for children to accurately write numbers in sequence. Creating a caterpillar for their own wall gives real purpose and personalisation too, and increases the likelihood that it will be used and referred to.

Taking it forward

- Provide ideas for caregivers that make use of the caterpillar as a poster. These may include: number recognition; the number that comes before/after; can you count on from this number? And guess my number.

What to do:

1. Set up an area with access to paints and gummed circles. Display the number cards in view of the area.

2. Demonstrate how to secure twelve circles, one at a time, slightly overlapping, into a long horizontal line resembling a caterpillar.

3. Emphasise careful counting as each circle is added, and have a final count to check again that there are twelve circles before the next part of the process begins.

4. Use the paint to create a face on the first circle on the left-hand side of the caterpillar.

5. Paint each number from 0–10 on the next 11 circles.

6. Invite the children to use this process to create a counting caterpillar.

7. Support children that require reminders with number sequence or formation.

8. Send each child home with their counting caterpillar for display on their bedroom wall.

Bead-string bag

Comparing and sequencing

What you need:

- Beads
- Pipe cleaners
- Scissors
- Fabric 'feely' bag

What to do:

1. Ahead of time, prepare the bead-strings to go into the feely bag.

2. Using the pipe cleaners and beads, begin with number one. Thread one bead onto a pipe cleaner, cut to size, and twist at both ends to secure.

3. Continue to thread two beads, three beads, and so on, until numbers one to ten are represented as bead-strings.

4. Place the bead-strings into the 'feely' bag.

5. Invite the children to put their hand into the bag to select a bead-string, one at a time. Can they guess which number they have selected using touch alone, without looking into the bag?

6. As the numbers are drawn from the bag, ask the children to arrange them in order from smallest to largest, or largest to smallest.

7. Finally, when the bag is empty, encourage the children check the order of the bead-strings by using them to count from one to ten, or ten to one.

What's in it for the children?

This experience creates a very visual representation of the number sequence between one and ten. By putting the numbers in order as they are randomly selected, the children are talking and thinking about comparison: 'Does this number come before or after? Is it bigger or smaller? What, if anything, remains missing in between?'

Taking it forward

- Provide cubes to enable children to create a 3D sequence using towers.

- Ask the children to draw their own pictures of the bead-strings to show which numbers are in the bag.

Is that a fact?

Number stories

What you need:

- Large sheets of paper and pens to record ideas or an interactive whiteboard
- Selection of identical items for counting (cubes or similar)
- Number line

Top tip ⭐

Use this opportunity to sensitively address misconceptions and incorrect use of language.

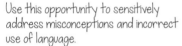

This is a great way to enable children to share their growing understanding of numbers and the number system. Showing and explaining thinking calls for accurate demonstration and use of appropriate number language. Comparing different means of showing and proving the same idea expands thinking and makes links between different areas of number knowledge.

Taking it forward

- Try suggesting facts to prompt the children if they are less confident.
- Use this activity to broaden and introduce new number language; interchange the use of 'larger and bigger'; 'equal and the same'.

What to do:

1. Ensure that the cubes or similar are placed within reach of the children for use when required.

2. Display a number line close enough that it can be referred to if required.

3. Choose a number that you wish to investigate with the children or ask a child to choose a number between a number boundary, e.g. one to ten.

4. Write the number in the centre of the paper or screen.

5. Ask the children to tell you everything that they know about the number.

6. Record each statement as it is made around the central number.

7. Using the cubes, number line, or with other resources in the setting, ask the children to prove each statement. How can they show that it is a fact?

8. Discuss and compare different ways of proving the same statement: 'Can anyone show this in a different way?'

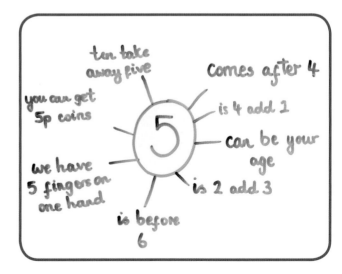

Cover it

What you need:

- Shallow bowl or small piece of fabric
- Counters (one colour only)

What's in it for the children?

This is a great introduction to developing knowledge that numbers can be partitioned in different ways, whilst the total amount remains the same. Children will initially return to zero and count from there, perhaps also using fingers to keep track of how many are covered. They will move on to use their knowledge of counting 'on from' or 'back from' to identify what is hidden and, over time, begin to apply recall of number bonds.

Taking it forward

- Invite individual children to take the lead, hiding amounts for the group.
- Remember to include experiences of zero, both zero on show and zero hidden.

What to do:

1. Explore this activity with a small group of children.

2. Select a number of counters, laying them in a group in full view of the children.

3. Invite the children to count how many altogether.

4. Ask the children to close their eyes whilst you take a small number of counters away and cover them with the bowl.

5. Ask the children to open their eyes and remind them of the number that was on display originally. Explain that some of the counters are under the bowl: can they say how many?

6. Talk through different ideas. Take time to allow children to explain how they reached their response.

7. Remove the bowl and count the hidden counters.

8. Recombine the counters, recounting the total one final time.

9. Repeat this process with the same number of counters a few times, choosing a different way to partition the number and concealing a different amount each time.

10. Repeat for different numbers of counters.

Domino match

Number stories

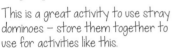

What you need:

- Selection of dominoes (sets are unnecessary)
- Number cards from 0–12 (or magnetic numbers)

Top tip ⭐

This is a great activity to use stray dominoes – store them together to use for activities like this.

What to do:

1. Arrange a collection of loose dominoes in a container.

2. Give the children the dominoes and a set of number cards.

3. Select a number card. Ask the children to find all of the dominoes with the corresponding number of spots.

4. Check at this point that the children are counting the total number of spots with accuracy. Model this if necessary, touching each spot whilst saying the number names in sequence.

5. Invite the children to work independently to match up the dominoes to the other number cards.

6. Can they find at least two different dominoes to match each number card?

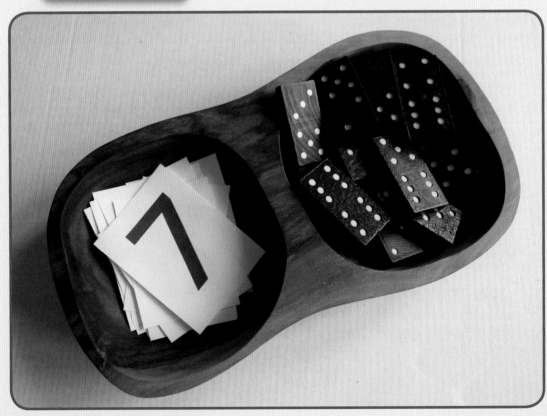

What's in it for the children?

This activity offers an opportunity to add two numbers together and to match the total to the corresponding written number. Encourage children to use the language of 'How many altogether?' and 'How many in total?'.

Taking it forward

- Give each child a small basket of dominoes to match to the corresponding number cards, encouraging them to organise the number cards in numerical order before beginning the domino sort.

- Use full sets of dominoes to play the traditional game.

What do you see?

Number stories

What you need:

- Whiteboard and pens, or an interactive whiteboard

Top tip

This is a great activity to utilise stray dominoes; store them together to use for activities like this.

What to do:

1. Display twelve identical coloured circles on the screen in a 3 x 4 grid pattern.

2. If using a whiteboard, use gummed paper circles or counters.

3. Gather the children together and ask, 'What do you see?'.

4. Talk through their ideas.

5. Ask them to fully explain their ideas and thoughts to the group as you annotate and move the circles, making them clear to everyone.

6. Make connections and comparisons between ideas: 'I can see 12; I can see three… We can see both!'

7. Move the 12 circles into two groups of six. 'What do you see?' Discuss ideas.

8. 'Can we move the circles into any other groups?'

9. Repeat the process with different numbers.

What's in it for the children?

Through this experience, children develop their understanding that a number can be viewed in different ways. It can be shared into groups; it can be partitioned into a variety of different sets. The very visual nature of the activity and the movement of the circles as they are taken apart and joined together in groups helps them to really 'see' this. Some children will quickly begin to see the commutativity of numbers, that 4 + 2 is the same as 2 + 4; others will take longer to make this connection.

Taking it forward

- Create a display of the activity, documenting the children's ideas within speech bubbles. It serves as a great reference point as they develop further knowledge of partitioning, number bonds and sharing.

- Repeat the activity, supplementing the whiteboard as a visual aid by giving each child the same number of beads to move and investigate themselves, as they share and listen to different ideas.

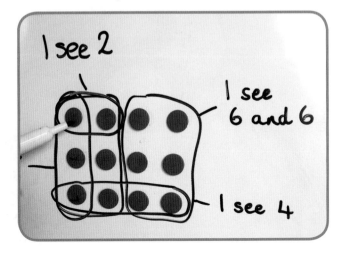

Race to the top
Adding and taking away

What you need:

- Cubes
- 1 large container
- Two identical containers
- Dice or number spinners

Taking it forward

- Try using pom-poms and tongs in place of cubes, or even smaller items, such as dried peas or beans.

- As they play the game a few times, ask children to use their own ways to record how many items the winner had in their cup: was it always the same number of items?

What to do:

1. Place the cubes in a central container.

2. Position two empty containers along with an accompanying dice or number spinner at each side of the central container.

3. Playing in pairs, explain to the children that the object of this game is to become the first person to fill their empty container to the top with cubes.

4. Ask the children to agree on a starting signal.

5. Begin the game, each child racing against the other, rolling or spinning, counting the corresponding number of cubes into the empty cup until one child reaches the top and declares themselves the winner.

6. Can the children empty their cups, line up and count their cubes comparing the number in each cup?

What's in it for the children?

This is a fun game to develop the concept that adding numbers together increases an amount. With experience, children develop an understanding that spinning or rolling larger numbers fills the cup more quickly.

More, more, more

Adding and taking away

What you need:

- Tower-building materials
  - blocks that join
  - cotton reels
  - cups
  - marshmallows
  - pebbles
  - shoe boxes
  - wooden blocks

What to do:

1. Set up play experiences, and encourage the children to create towers with the materials.

2. Challenge the children to add more, until their tower reaches the highest point it can without toppling over.

3. Work with them to rebuild fallen towers, adding one at a time, and taking one away as they begin to wobble.

4. Talk with the children as they build and experiment, using the language of addition, subtraction and comparison.

Top tip ⭐

Try to avoid firing questions, shoehorning in mathematical language and giving instructions as the children play. Be much more discrete about the intended learning and let the children guide the activity.

What's in it for the children?

This is a very visual exploration of adding more to increase, and taking away to leave less. It offers an opportunity for discussion using addition and subtraction terms, such as 'add, one more, bigger/large/higher, smaller/lower, take, fewer, one less, and the terms of comparison such as, nearly, almost, the same and equal'.

Taking it forward

- Invite the children to draw pictures of the towers: can they label each part with a number?

Add one, take one

Adding and taking away

What you need:

- Plain rectangular card
- Pens
- Gold coins
- Counters
- Dice

What's in it for the children?

This is a game to develop counting skills and to develop understanding that adding increases a number, whilst taking away causes it to decrease. Players become very aware of this cause and effect, as they strive to collect the highest number of gold coins to enable them to win the game.

Taking it forward

- Create different versions of the gameboard, marked with adding and taking either one, two or three gold coins, increasing the jeopardy as play unfolds!

What to do:

1. Prepare the gameboard in advance. Do this by drawing a looped track onto the card and dividing it into sections. Mark a START and FINISH square. Mark each of the remaining squares either ADD 1 or TAKE 1.

2. The gameboard can be decorated and laminated at this stage, although this isn't necessary for playing the game.

3. The aim of the game is to be the one with the highest number of gold coins when the game ends.

4. To begin, each player must count out ten gold coins from a coin bank and select a counter, positioning this on the START square on the track.

5. Players take turns to roll the dice, move their counter the corresponding number of squares, and follow the instructions in the square they land on – either taking away or adding to their gold coins.

6. The game ends when the first player reaches the FINISH square. Each player counts their gold coins; the person with the most wins.

7. If a player finds themselves with no gold coins and the game is still in play, they cannot continue play and are out of the game.

Top tip ★

Non-readers will need help with the words 'add' and 'take' initially, but they will quickly start to recognise them as sight words.

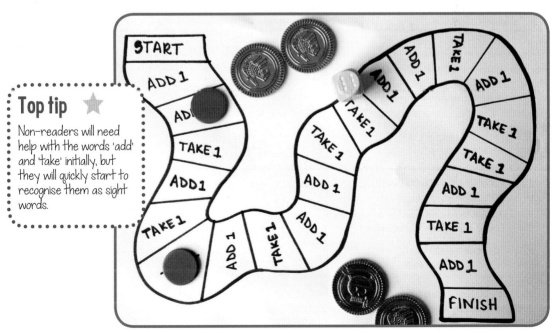

Beanbag throw

Adding and taking away

What you need:

- Number beanbags 1–10 and basket to hold them
- Container big enough to throw beanbags into
- Counters

What's in it for the children?

This is a game that reinforces correspondence between a number and a representative amount and develops children's experience of combining small groups to count how many altogether. Playing with others, rather than using this activity independently, introduces number comparison, as the player with the highest total overall wins the game.

Taking it forward

- To simplify the game, ask players to take one counter for each beanbag thrown into the container, rather than the amount corresponding to the number shown on the beanbag.

- Play the game in two teams with the whole group. Represent on-going scores on a whiteboard, allowing opportunities for number comparison after every turn. This may become highly competitive!

What to do:

1. Place the beanbags in a basket.
2. Set up the container and beanbags a short distance from each other in the room.
3. Invite children to play this game in pairs or small groups of three.
4. Each child takes it in turn to select a beanbag, without looking at its number, from the basket.
5. Can they throw the beanbag into the container? If their beanbag makes it in, the child counts out and keeps the corresponding number of counters; if it misses the container, they do not receive any counters.
6. Return beanbags that have not made it into the container back to the basket as the game is played.
7. Play until all beanbags are thrown into the container.
8. Each child adds up their total number of counters.
9. The child with the highest number of counters wins the game.

Reading the signs
Adding and taking away

What you need:
- Sticky notes
- Three shallow bowls
- Cubes or similar items for counting

What's in it for the children?

This offers a practical opportunity to create, read, interpret and solve an equation using the signs. This activity assumes knowledge of each sign and experience of addition and subtraction.

Taking it forward

- Encourage the children to create their own plus, minus and equals sticky notes.
- Provide materials to enable the children to record some of their number sentences.

What to do:
1. Take three sticky notes; mark them with an addition, subtraction and equals sign.
2. Set out the three bowls in a row, allowing space between for the sticky notes.
3. Demonstrate the activity to the children.
4. Choose either addition or subtraction. Place a number of cubes into each bowl; add corresponding sticky notes, and read the number sentence with the children.
5. Talk with the children as you move cubes accordingly and work out the solution, adding cubes to the final bowl to complete the number sentence.
6. Re-read the completed number sentence. Repeat for different examples.
7. Invite the children to explore the activity independently.

Top tip ⭐

Often children will have been introduced to these signs outside the setting. Though it may not be a priority within your learning goals at this stage to ensure that every child can read and interpret the signs, don't hold back children who have experience of addition and subtraction, knowledge of the signs and an interest in investigating them in this way.

Empty!

Adding and taking away

What you need:

- Two identical cups or bowls
- Cubes or similar counting material in two colours
- Two number spinners or dice
- Counters

What to do:

1. Count an identical number of cubes into each cup; aim for around 20. Select a different colour of cube for each cup, ensuring this game is self-managing for the children.

2. Children play this game in pairs.

3. Provide each child with a filled cup and spinner or dice.

4. To play the game, children race against each other, spinning their spinner, taking the corresponding number of cubes out of the cup, repeating until one child shouts, 'Empty!'.

5. Each time the game ends, the winning child collects a counter and the cubes are tipped back into each cup.

6. Play the game a few times, collecting counters, until the children decide to stop.

7. The winner has the highest total number of counters overall.

What's in it for the children?

Playing the game reinforces the process of subtraction as one of a small number being taken from a bigger number, creating a very visual representation of an amount decreasing until only zero remains.

Taking it forward

- Ask the children to count how many cubes were left in the cup of the child who has not won. How close were they to winning?

- Encourage the children to count the cubes back into the cup as they begin the game again.

Four in a row
Adding and taking away

What you need:

- Plain card
- Ruler
- Pen
- Spotty dice
- Cubes or other counting aid
- Counters

What's in it for the children?

This game offers an opportunity to practise combining two amounts to find a total. The children will initially touch and count each spot on both dice to find the total. They will progress to count on from one dice, adding the other, and finally use their increasing knowledge of dice patterns to identify the numbers without counting and their knowledge of number bonds to add them together. Which of these addition strategies is used will depend entirely on their level of knowledge and experience.

Taking it forward

- Extend the length of the game, playing until all of the numbers on one card are covered. Winner shouts, 'bingo'.

- Use numbered dice or a 1–9 number spinner, rather than spotty dice.

What to do:

1. Using card, create at least four game cards. Each should measure approximately 16 x 16 cm in size.

2. Divide each card into a grid of 16 equal squares.

3. Choosing random numbers between two and 12, write a number in each square, creating a bingo-style card for each player. Laminate at this stage for longer use if desired.

4. Play the game in pairs or small groups.

5. Each player takes a turn to roll two dice and add the numbers together. Encourage the children to work together, supporting each other with this step if required. They may also like to use cubes for assistance.

6. If the total number rolled is found on the player's gamecard, it can be covered with a counter.

7. Players continue to take turns, until one player has four counters in a row, winning the game.

Missing treasure

Adding and taking away

What you need:

- Treasure chest or bowl
- 10–15 gold coins 'treasure'
- Props to represent a pirate (an eye patch, pirate hat or waistcoat work well)
- 'Loot' bag

What to do:

1. Gather together the chest, coins and pirate props. The scale of the chest and the treasure will depend on whether this game is to be accessed independently by small groups of children or played with a larger adult-led group.

2. Begin by asking the children to fill the chest with the coins, counting each item as it is added, to find the total.

3. Choose a child to act as the pirate. Invite them to use the dressing-up props.

4. All children close their eyes whilst the pirate steals some coins from the chest, hiding it inside the loot bag.

5. Have the pirate to call on the other children to open their eyes when their raid is complete.

6. Can we find out how much treasure is missing?

7. Encourage the children to work together to find out how much has been taken.

8. Encourage discussion and sharing of ideas and strategies. Counting forwards from the number that remains to reach the original total number, whilst keeping track on fingers, will reveal the missing number. Model this if the children require support.

9. Make statements and ask questions to support thinking: 'There are three left over; there were seven; does that tell us four coins are missing?'

10. Now ask the pirate to empty the loot bag, counting out the stolen treasure.

11. Gather the coins together, choose a different pirate, and begin the game again.

What's in it for the children?

This is an ideal game for the children to use the language of taking away, and to explore strategies to count how many remain, and work out how many are missing. The decrease in amount every time coins are taken reinforces understanding that a number gets smaller when an amount is taken away.

Taking it forward

- Make gold or silver coins with the children, rather than preparing in advance.

- Decrease the number of coins for less-experienced children.

- Have a treasure hunt within your setting. Hide ten supersize gold coins and challenge the children to beat the timer to return them to the chest. There must be ten in total before the timer runs out.

Number 10 bus

Adding and taking away

What you need:

- Plain card
- Counters if required

Top tip

Depending on the experience of the children, the passengers on their bus may not always accurately represent the number in the story being told. This is a great activity to enable this type of observational assessment.

What's in it for the children?

This gives a familiar context to practise both adding and taking away, according to the events described in an imaginary situation. Using positional language to describe where the passengers are sitting adds another mathematical dimension to this activity.

Taking it forward

- Give a child the role of storyteller.

- Play a life-sized version with seats arranged in rows and a seat for the driver at the front. Tell the story as the children get on and off the bus.

What to do:

1. Cut the card into rectangular base cards. You will require one per child.

2. Either by hand, or using a computer package, create a ten-frame grid within a surrounding image of a double decker bus for each card.

3. Using card, make ten circular faces (passengers) for each base card. These should fit inside the square 'windows' on the ten frame. Counters could be used in place of these circular faces.

4. Begin the activity by giving each child a bus and access to the 'passenger' faces or counters.

5. Talk with the children about the scenario of a bus journey; discuss the driver, tickets, stops, routes and their own personal experiences.

6. Explain to the children that they are going to take on the role of bus driver, driving the number 10 bus.

7. Begin telling the story of the bus's journey. Describe the number of passengers getting on or off the bus at each stop.

8. As the story is told, each child adds or takes away 'passengers' from their bus base card.

9. Ask questions as the journey progresses: 'How many passengers are left on the bus. If 3 passengers got on, and then another 3, how many are on the bus altogether?'

10. Continue adding and taking away passengers, creating a surrounding story until, finally, all passengers leave the bus empty as it returns to the garage at the end of the day.

Skittles

Adding and taking away

What's in it for the children?

As the game is played, children have an opportunity to reinforce number recognition and counting out corresponding small amounts. Successful players see their score growing before their eyes, as they collect and add to their total. More-experienced children will begin to make size comparisons between scores, using approximation as the game progresses.

Taking it forward

- For less-experienced children, play the game with unmarked bottles, collecting one counter for each bottle knocked over.

What to do:

1. Rinse and remove any labels from each bottle.

2. Mark each bottle clearly in the centre with a number from 1–5 using a broad permanent marker pen, or by attaching a numbered label.

3. To aid stability, fill each bottle with water or dry sand until you reach a level that you are satisfied with; this will depend on the size and shape of the bottles. Test one by setting it around a metre away and rolling the ball, attempting to knock it over. Too heavy and this will be impossible, too light and the bottles will not be stable enough to create a satisfactory game.

4. Gather the children and demonstrate how to play 'skittles' using the bottles and ball.

5. Identify an appropriate distance between the skittles and bowling spot with the children, suiting their age and stage. Mark this on the floor with tape.

6. Explain that each player has two turns to roll the ball, returning the skittles to their places after the first turn.

7. After both rolls, the player collects the number of counters that correspond with the numbers on the skittles that have been knocked over.

8. All skittles are then replaced, ready for the next player.

9. End the game after each player has taken three turns (of two rolls). All players count how many counters they have collected altogether, and the player with the highest number wins.

What you need:

- Dough
- Dough tools
  - rolling pins
  - knives
  - rotating cutters
- Containers divided into sections (collect these from food packaging)

What's in it for the children?

As the children play, they are exploring what it means to share one whole into a number of smaller parts. The challenge encourages them to investigate how to make sharing fair, to use the language and concepts of comparison and sharing: enough, not enough, less, more, the same, not the same, all, some, and equal.

Taking it forward

- Provide scales or balance pans to further develop exploration of sharing equally.
- Replace the containers with a set of play plates or bowls.

What to do:

1. Set up the dough and containers as an invitation to play and explore.
2. Play alongside the children, encouraging them to divide the dough between the different sections within the containers.

Using one container…

3. Can they share so that every part of the container has some dough in it?
4. Is it possible to share so that every part has the same or equal amount of dough?
5. Are there different ways to share the dough equally? 'Show me how!'

Pouring and filling

Sharing

What you need:

- Variety of containers
- Water
- Different sized-jugs and pourers; include some with scales
- Food colouring

What's in it for the children?

Engaging in water play using these limited materials focuses the children on sharing and dividing a larger amount into smaller amounts. By playing alongside the children as they experiment, you can encourage them to use and develop the language of sharing and division. Offering a challenge develops awareness and understanding of the idea of equal amounts.

Taking it forward

- Replace water with dry pouring materials: beans, lentils, small beads, dry sand.
- Provide funnels to add extra interest.

What to do:

1. Set out the materials as an open-ended exploration.
2. Allow the children plenty of time to play and explore independently.
3. Limit the amount of water. Add colour to emphasise the small amount available.
4. Play alongside the children or set them a challenge.
5. Can you share the water between all of the containers?
6. What could we do to make sure each of the containers has an equal quantity of water?
7. Allow time for the children to explore these ideas, and if they have worked independently, make time to discuss what they were doing and noticing as they completed the challenge.

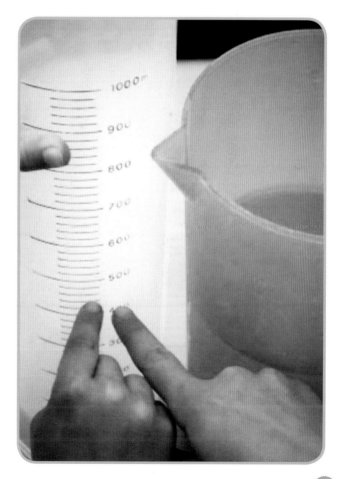

Fruit salad

Sharing

What you need:

- Selection of fresh fruit
- Chopping boards
- Child-safe knives (available online)
- Bowls

What to do:

1. Discuss the selection of fruit with the children.

2. Explain that some of the fruit is going to be cut into pieces and used to make a fruit salad for everyone to enjoy.

3. Identify how many people are going to eat the fruit salad.

4. Ask the children to decide which fruit will be used. They may wish to gather information about the likes and dislikes of the group.

5. 'How many of each fruit will we need to use?'

6. Discuss the way that each fruit will be cut and prepared, and explore how many pieces or portions each fruit will provide. You may wish to demonstrate this with each type of fruit.

7. Discuss and compare the number of pieces that each fruit will provide with the number of children eating the fruit salad.

8. Support the children to prepare and portion the fruit salad for the group.

✚ Health & Safety

Elements of this activity may be adult-only tasks. Ensure that risk assessments and allergy awareness are in place.

What's in it for the children?

Making a fruit salad provides an everyday context to explore sharing whole fruits by cutting into pieces, to combine the pieces to create a whole (fruit salad), and then to share once more as the whole fruit salad is divided between the group.

Taking it forward

- Offer writing materials as the children may wish to create signs or menus showing different fruits and the number of portions available.

- Ask the children to reflect together on whether the activity was a success: did they have enough to go around; what would they do differently next time?

- Try this with other food contexts: pancakes, vegetables and dips.

Questions, questions

What you need:

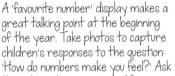

- Materials to note responses

Top tip ⭐

A 'favourite number' display makes a great talking point at the beginning of the year. Take photos to capture children's responses to the question: 'How do numbers make you feel?' Ask them to make exaggerated faces which can be printed and annotated with their thoughts.

What's in it for the children?

Number is often explored and taught as something quite removed from feelings or opinions, and yet when asked, children usually have strong feelings and ideas about numbers. Shared discussion, particularly when focusing on what children wonder or would like to find out about number, develops a sense of having a go and takes away the sense that numbers are something to be learned about through instruction only. Responses to the questions provide great information to inform future planning and great insight into the children's level of confidence with number. They generate useful starting points to engage children in their future learning.

Taking it forward

- Document responses to the questions in a giant 'number book' for use in future sessions.
- Choose one question as a central theme and create a wall display as a talking point.
- Send the questions home and invite responses to be brought in and shared with the whole group.

What to do:

1. Talk with the children using the questions below as focus for discussion. You may decide to take one question and explore it in depth with the whole group, or to use the question as the basis for work with a small group.

    - How do numbers make you feel?
    - What's your favourite number? Why?
    - What do you know about numbers?
    - What do you wonder about numbers?
    - What would you like to find out about numbers?
    - Are there any numbers that you don't like?
    - What is the biggest number that you know?
    - What are numbers for?
    - Who do you think uses numbers?